Learning Fun

YOUNG & GIFTED SERIES

This book belongs to:

_____

LADDER
CLIMBERS

One Blue Circle

Two Green Triangles

2

Three Red Squares

3

Four purple Diamonds

Five Orange Stars

Six Black Rectangles

6

Seven pink Hearts

7

Eight Brown Hexagons

Nine Yellow Pentagons

9

↑↑↑↑↑
↑↑↑↑↑

Ten Gray Arrows

10 ↑

A a

A is for Apple

B b

B is for Banana

C is for Carrot

D d

D is for Dog

E e

E is for Elephant

F f

F is for Frog

G g

G is for Giraffe

H h

H is for Horse

Ii

I is for Ice

J j

J is for Juice

K k

K is for Kangaroo

L is for Lion

M m

M is for Moon

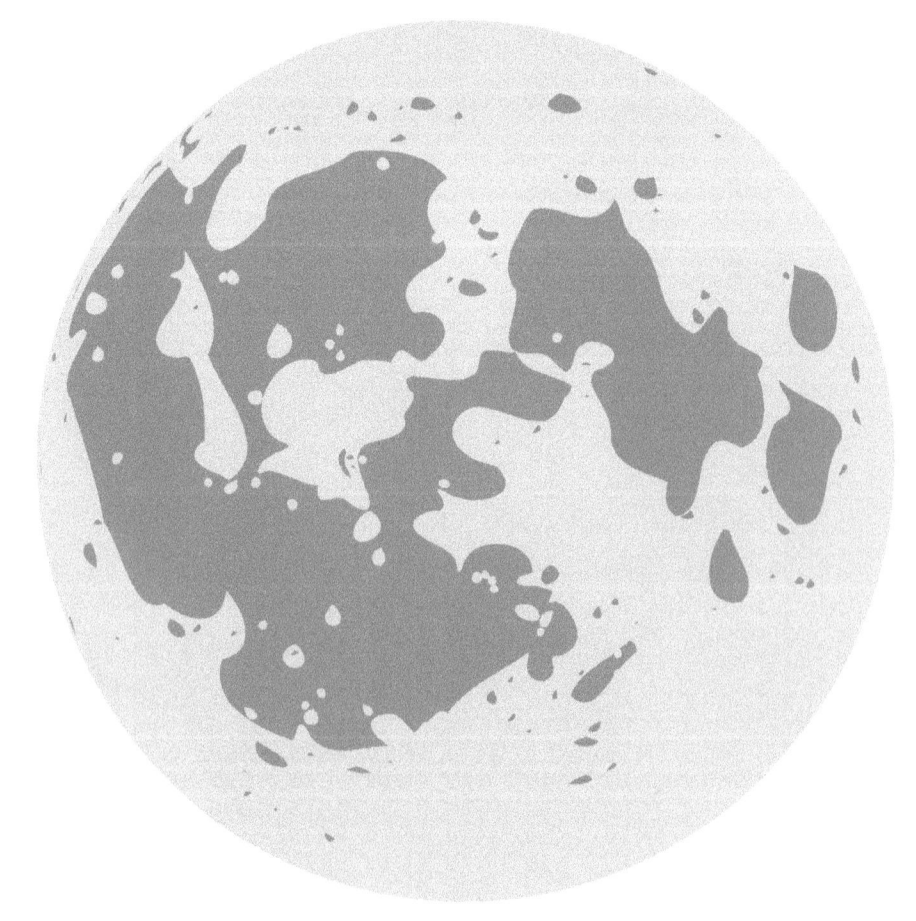

N n

N is for Nickel

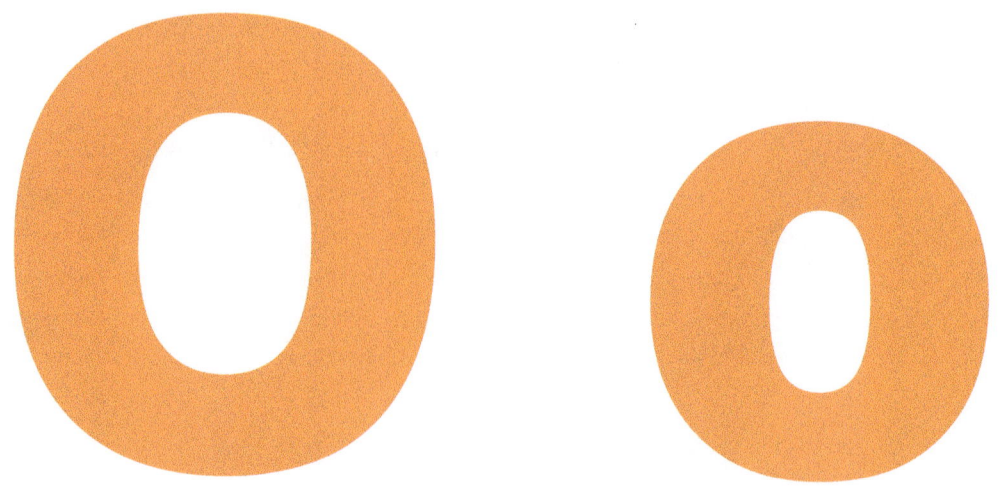

O is for orange

P p

p is for pig

Q is for Quilt

R r

R is for Raccoon

S s

S is for Snail

T t

T is for Tree

U u

U is for umbrella

V v

V is for Van

W w

w is for whale

x is for xylophone

Y y

Y is for Yo-Yo

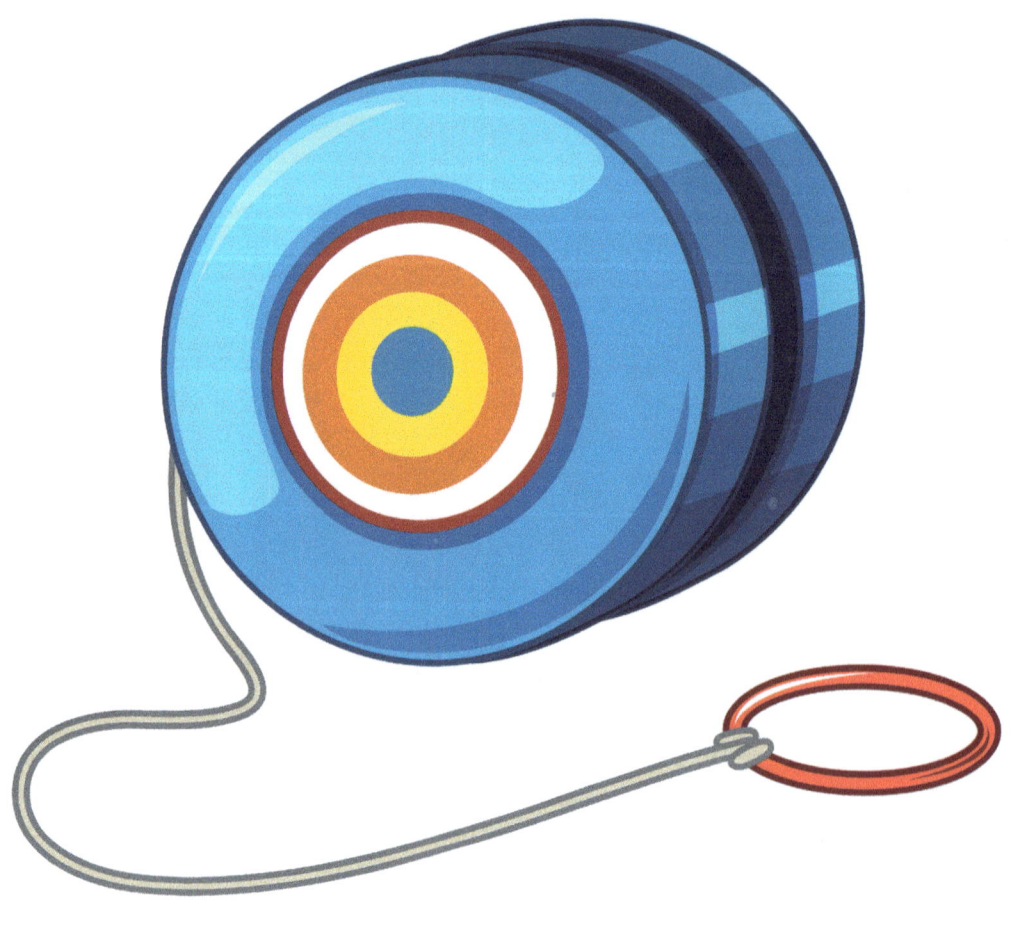

Z z

z is for zebra

LADDER
CLIMBERS